FATHER AND SON
The Selected Poems of F.R. Higgins

F.R. Higgins

FATHER AND SON

The Selected Poems of F.R. Higgins

ARLEN
HOUSE

Father and Son
The Selected Poems of F.R. Higgins

is published in 2014 by
ARLEN HOUSE
42 Grange Abbey Road
Baldoyle,
Dublin 13,
Ireland
Phone/Fax: 353–86–8207617
Email: arlenhouse@gmail.com
arlenhouse.blogspot.com

978–1–85132–081–3, paperback
978–1–85132–091–2, hardback

Distributed internationally by
SYRACUSE UNIVERSITY PRESS
621 Skytop Road, Suite 110
Syracuse, NY 13244–5290, USA
Phone: 315–443–5534/Fax: 315–443–5545
Email: supress@syr.edu

Original selection of poems by R. Dardis Clarke
Editing by Joseph Woods, Alan Hayes and Aidan Gray

Typesetting ¦ Arlen House

CONTENTS

from *Arable Holdings* (1933)

from *The Gap of Brightness* (1940)

Uncollected Poems (1926–1939) from *The Dublin Magazine*

In memory of R. Dardis Clarke

INTRODUCTION

Joseph Woods

This book serves to reintroduce and make available the poetry of F.R. Higgins (1896–1941), and to remember R. Dardis Clarke (1939–2013).

Dardis Clarke was a passionate supporter of poets and poetry, and in particular the poetry of F.R. Higgins. At the time of his death, which took us all by surprise and sorrow in February of this year, Dardis was finalising a second edition of Higgins' poetry. Of late he was working with Aidan Gray, a relative of Higgins and whose family continue to live in Higginsbrook, the elegant house in Meath which Higgins has immortalised and where he spent much of his childhood.

For those who didn't know him, Dardis Clarke was a larger than life character, ebullient, bohemian and passionate, cutting a dash wherever he walked, a genial Karl Marx look-alike, always suited in black with an open-necked black shirt regardless of the weather and a fedora-style, broad-rimmed leather hat.

He appeared open to everyone and the world and greeted people with a bellow, bear hug or embrace and, at the same time, lived his life in compartments and could be secretive and even shy. Many of his wide network of friends met for the first time at his funeral, a humanist service full of poetry and poets, journalists and trade unionists and people representing all of the many facets of Dublin life, in which the President, An Uachtaráin Michael D. Higgins quietly attended. It was apparent to all, that in Dardis' departure, Dublin had lost a true soul of the city and some of her own soul.

Some of Dardis' traits have been compared to his father, the poet Austin Clarke, but Dardis was his own man and took from his father an enduring loyalty to poetry, and in turn to his own father's reputation. In 2008 he compiled and edited the *Collected Poems of Austin Clarke*, a book that took many years of work and dedication; it followed upon *Austin Clarke Remembered: Essays, Poems and Reminiscences to Mark the Centenary of His Birth* in 1996.

According to Maurice Harmon, Dardis set out to do the *Collected* because he was upset with the typographical errors in the original edition from 1974. His professional background as a journalist made him an excellent proof-reader and, despite some peculiarities of style – he hated the ampersand – he had his own house style, which in turn became the house style of *Poetry Ireland Review*. He proofed every copy of the *Review* from as far back as anyone can remember. In addition, he served on the Board of Poetry Ireland, was a past Chairman and uniquely attended almost every Poetry Ireland reading. A familiar and welcome sight at the back of the room and, more often than once, he was the audience. When the audience was more than a half-dozen he always did a discrete head count and reported it at the end of each reading.

Poetry Ireland, in collaboration with Aidan Gray of Higginsbrook, and Alan Hayes of Arlen House, has decided to honour his memory and his loyalty by completing his last project, bringing this planned book to publication.

On the centenary of F.R. Higgins' birth, Dardis wrote an investigative article on Higgins for *The Irish Times* in which he tracked down his place of work, his Trade Union activity, and an account of meeting his widow Beatrice May Higgins, and ultimately, visiting Higgins' final resting place in his beloved Laracor in the County Meath of his forefathers. This was a rare foray, certainly for Dardis, to actually leave Dublin; he maintained a healthy distrust of the countryside and of people from outside Dublin! In this he was like his father Austin, who once described himself as a 'town mouse'.

Dardis eventually followed up his interest by privately publishing F.R. Higgins' *The 39 Poems*, selected and edited by R. Dardis Clarke in 1992. What was most unusual in this edition was that he revived the imprint of 'The Bridge Press'; this imprint had been used by his father to publish verse plays and limited editions of his own poems. Dardis revived both the imprint and returned Higgins to print for the first time in fifty years. The book contained selections from all four poetry collections of Higgins.

Twenty years later, with this edition long out of print, Dardis decided it was time again to republish Higgins with a wider selection. This time he drew on additional poems and also a series of 'strays' or poems that appeared in *The Dublin Magazine* in which Higgins was one of the most prolific poetry contributors. The selection was essentially a more generous and comprehensive gathering than the previous volume; in all a total of sixty poems from 1923 to 1940, the year before the poet's death.

Frederick Robert Higgins (1896–1941) was born in Foxford, Co. Mayo and attended school there, with summers in Meath in his beloved Higginsbrook; both of his parents had come from Meath. He left school at fourteen and by the age of sixteen was working as a clerk in Dublin for Brooks Thomas, a builders' firm. He became active in the Labour movement and founded a Clerical Workers Union which resulted in his dismissal from employment. As well as being a Trade Unionist he also had strong nationalist leanings and resisted pressure from his father, a Protestant Unionist, to enlist in the First World War. This apparently caused a rift between them.

Higgins then began editing magazines and continued to do so for the rest of his life. Among them, he established a pioneering women's magazine in Ireland, which only lasted two issues; the first issue entitled *Welfare* and the second *Farewell*. In 1915 he became friends with Austin Clarke, both were born within a few weeks of each other; each encouraged the other in their enthusiasm for folklore, Gaelic literature and the art of the early Irish church.

In 1921 he married Beatrice May Moore whom he had met in Brooks Thomas. She was a fine harpist and would work with Higgins on magazine editing. In 1923 Higgins published a chapbook entitled *Salt Air* and began publishing regularly in journals; his first book *Island Blood* would follow in 1925 and in all he would publish four books of poetry.

In 1932, tired of city life, Higgins and his wife Beatrice decided to leave Dublin to spend a year in the West of Ireland in an attempt, according to Austin Clarke, to catch the last of disappearing traditional life. They choose a cottage overlooking Lough Conn, opposite Mount Nephin, a mountain mentioned in many Gaelic love poems of the past. Remote as the cottage was, it was only seven miles from Foxford where Higgins was born; their one-year there grew into three.

On their return to Dublin, they eventually settled into a house on the Lower Dodder Road, Rathfarnham, and it was to this house that W.B. Yeats called one day and arranged an appointment with Beatrice for Higgins to come and visit him at Riversdale. Riversdale was hardly a mile up the road and thus began a close friendship that would last until Yeats' death in 1939.

Higgins was elected a foundation member of the Irish Academy of Letters and in 1935 became a director of the Abbey Theatre. That same year, with the encouragement of Yeats, he had his only play, a one-act verse play *A Deuce O' Jacks* based on the life of Dublin ballad-maker Zozimus, performed at the Abbey. He also edited with Yeats a series of broadside ballads for the Cuala Press.

In 1937 the Abbey Players toured the US and Canada and Higgins managed the whole project with perhaps fatal consequences for his health. He returned to Ireland in 1938, a worn-out man. He was now Managing Director of the Abbey and was plagued with ill-health and presumably heart disease.

When his last book, *The Gap of Brightness*, was published in 1940 and received a very favourable review in *The Irish Times*, the editor R.M. Smyllie and a close friend of Higgins had a poster of it made and one was brought to his bed. When he saw it, he dressed and went into town for one last reunion with friends. He asked his old friend Brinsley MacNamara 'when you go down to Laracor again, put your arms round the land for me'.

F.R. Higgins died a few days later at the age of forty-four and was buried with his father under a yew tree in the churchyard in Laracor. On his grave are the lines, taken from 'Father and Son', 'With whom now he is one, under yew branches'.

F.R. Higgins' poetry is that of a meticulous craftsman; heavily influenced initially by an immersion in Douglas Hyde's book of translations, *The Love Songs of Connacht*, which in turn was a source book for the entire Literary Revival.

In his first book *Island Blood* (1925) there is a clear flavour of what is to come from his keen metrical ear to his ballad style. It has been suggested that Higgins often composed to the rhythm of Irish airs and ballad tunes and consequently when the poem was finished the tune was discarded but the lyric retained. 'Island Blood', the eponymous poem, is a clear example of Higgins' complex rhyming patterns that also included repeating certain words. He and Austin Clarke were substituting Gaelic vowel rhymes – assonances – for conventional rhymes and this innovation had a huge effect on Higgins' verse. He continues in this vein two years later with the publication of *The Dark Breed* (1927) that includes the sensually charged 'Poachers' and 'A Tinker's Woman'. However, the project of marrying complex rhyming patterns to the movement of song sometimes makes the poetry appear in a hurry, exuberant and often overloaded with rich phrasing, and occasionally the author is absent.

A shift comes about in his next two books, *Arable Holdings* (1933) and *Gap of Brightness* (1940). Here can be found Higgins' better-known anthology favourites; 'Father and Son', 'The Old Jockey', 'Padraic O'Conaire – Gaelic Story-Teller', 'The Boyne Walk', 'Auction' (which Brian Fallon, who has written excellently on Higgins' poetry, regarded as his finest) and a personal favourite, the orientally sparse and indeed minimalist 'Chinese Winter' – Austin Clarke mentions that as early as 1915, Higgins was discoursing on Japanese poetry. It's worth noting that despite Higgins' books being long out of print, a handful of his poems continued to appear in anthologies, with his most popular 'Father and Son' appearing in *The Irish Times Book of Favourite Irish Poems* (Dublin, 2000), chosen by the Irish public.

'Father and Son' was unusual for Higgins in that it dealt directly with a personal theme and, as he explained to Padraic Fallon, he had discovered a new kind of easy poetry movement. In the same batch of poems you could also include 'Exhortation' as indicative of where Higgins' poetic direction might have developed. Curiously, as Higgins was testing new waters and perhaps reconsidering folksong and its effects in his latter years, it was at a time when Yeats wanted specifically to become a popular poet and to write songs for the people. He called on Higgins, and Yeats' later poems have a racy ballad quality which benefited greatly from Higgins' own work and earthy influence.

Whether or not Higgins would have re-invented himself in middle-age, as poets hope to, will never be seen, but he will be remembered for his elegies, for his evocation of quiet but royal Meath, and for the west and its people.

Unusually, he haunted both east and west of the country, with 'Chinese Winter', inclining him further east again. Through this book, and Dardis Clarke's selection, I hope his work finds the foothold it merits.

FATHER AND SON

The Selected Poems of F.R. Higgins

from
Island Blood
(London, John Lane, The Bodley Head, 1925)

THE OLD WINE

Of all the grace in song –
    The faintly coloured grace –
We know sweet airs belong
    To your sweet face;
And even subtle art,
    With light and dainty line,
Can only tell in part
    Or faintly define
Your body's timid rhythm
    In light steps or grave;
For such ease is with them
    That they please the courtly fashions
Of a Helen or a Maeve.

I heard a beggar toy
    The pavements with his stave,
And lift his voice for joy
    And love of Maeve;
The flush of Helen's wine
    On ghostly nudities,
On cold men herding swine
    By wasted seas,
Was captured in his singing –
    But where's Beauty's joy,
While Beauty's dust is clinging
    To a lonely cairn in Connacht
And a burning wind from Troy.

Then let us play an air
    Upon the well-tuned string –
While wind-blown orchards bare
    The sweets of Spring,
And chasing black winds stain
    The grassy pools at eve;

Come, tip the strings again
   And slowly weave
Praise to immortal Beauty
   In old songs strung anew,
For it's music's duty
   That, while praising Maeve and Helen,
Beauty's echo praises you!

THE YOUNG MAN

O would I could leave lime stones and all grey kilns,
    As I walk wet with the evening through hard grass,
Watching hawks fall from their standing above the fresh hills
    And with them tasting the sea's taste as swallows pass!

O to live where the sea lives and under a long green bough
    That even in calm clear days is twisting a breeze;
And to lead from the blackbird fields just one young cow,
    Fat as a snail in the moon-tide and silked like the seas!

By Hell, I will gallop there soon on a clean grey mare,
    With the world's weight flung away from my wild feet,
And I lifting a cheer, over Bohernabreena's fair,
    From sweat-lit athletes and the gleemen that compete!

If breweries be hived in the bloom of June's chill sap,
    Come, men with the lime-stinging lips; cut high your goodbyes:
For maybe my slim ship grows from the wood's dark lap
    Or a mating, fresh girl with perilous lakes in her eyes!

CONNEMARA

The soft rain is falling
   Round bushy isles,
Veiling the waters
   Over wet miles,
And hushing the grasses
   Where plovers call,
While soft clouds are falling
   Over all.

I pulled my new curragh
   Through the clear sea
And left the brown sailings
   Far behind me,
For who would not hurry
   Down to the isle,
Where Una has lured me
   With a smile.

She moves through her sheiling
   Under the haws,
Her movements are softer
   Than kitten's paws;
And shiny blackberries
   Sweeten the rain,
Where I haunt her beaded
   Window-pane.

I would she were heeding –
   Keeping my tryst –
That soft moon of amber
   Blurred in the mist,
And raising the plovers
   Where salleys fall,

Till slumbers come hushing
    One and all.

WISDOM

O who will say he is wise
   When he hears a bird sing,
When he looks with seeing eyes
   On a butterfly's wing;
Or play to the world's pride,
   Who looks on the waters where
An old pike rubs his side
   In the rocks near Dromahaire.

Come away to this holy air,
   Where birds cheer every tree
On the roads round Dromahaire
   Hooded with greenery;
Come away to this simple lake
   And learn at the voice of a bird
To vie with the music and make
   New worlds in a word.

DRUMMIN WOOD

As bare as a salley on the autumn waters
After red moonrise,
And as bright as the eye of a hunting otter
While the salmon lies,
She comes in the quiet of unseen dewfall –
Lightly, quietly avoiding the dewfall,
Into the wood she flies.

Ah, I fear she will frighten the little red foxes
From their ferny lair,
And that squirrel out on the juicy branches,
Sniffing the wholesome air;
But she lightly treads as if treading on blossoms –
The dead trees are bursting again in blossoms,
As she is stepping there.

O, I would we could wander while the blue stars glimmer
Through the salmon's abode;
O, to quietly wander where the fruitful hazels
Bear each unripe load
Above the rocks by the blue lake waters –
Lovers wandering down by the waters
On a shining sandy road!

CLEOPATRA
'Thou dost renew thyself, O thou most beautiful being'
The Book of the Dead

The white censer of your ripe body
Swings to this old worship,
And drunken I follow the rich waves
Of your dance in a sheiling of Connacht,
Without fiddle, nor cymbal, nor zither
Slipped from your green shawl to bare skin
This stark night –
Limbs whipped by fantastical turf-light.

O spin wild hips on ankles belled in gold,
Nor rest the keen breasts, as mushrooms meshed in grasses,
While pregnant with the summer's riot, those starving paps
Hunger for the mouthless joys.

Ebbed shoreless by your eyes' tormenting moons,
A visionary darkness flames the mind –
Ebbed shoreless –
Of sun-strewn navies, ragged in each wind,
And that lone bird, whose fiery revival,
Throws your beauty over half a world.

Yes, dance an immortal delight, just to-night,
Without fiddle, nor cymbal, nor zither,
As my dreams drift cloudwise round your world,
Beyond the grassy door, beyond the dew
Into blind woods;
And through their burning night
Slim sliver eels weave shivering watery light,
And animals of sleepy sinews move.

The boughs of ancient orchards blossom through your skin,
Lost winds are in your swaying,

As away on your dancing ways I go
By Mayo's bushy shores in the sloe glens,
Dark lass of the Pharaohs, by grass-sown waters
Pulling, as we pass the royal Boyne,
Sunless rushes from a world of cloud and stone,
Flag leaves for our naked bed,
Where poised air pillaring the dumb hawk shatters
And gathers song.

Then ravish with dances my nude eyes to-night,
Keen limbs from the blue quilts of Egypt –
Body agile, yet taut, too lithe for the flail
Of curling sweet thongs in the love thresh;
From a fox's skull, for you, I claw ripe honey
I tear thick fat milk from the she-hare's side,
Then taste within my mouth the breath of forests,
The strength of mountains from my virile love –
For we are carven from the rocky sun,
High comrades with bright Ra and Aengus,
Companions with Houris and Lugh,
Hailing from the mildewed throat of darkness
Grey-cairned and tomb-graven loves.

Thus, love, in our love the dull years become
Just one delirious Spring,
From Brugh na Boinne, through the brightening rushes
To the green airy Nile, grown passionate,
Dreaming from its black heart;
In that fire of ghostly lovers and your dead stars
My limbs knit with the skies,
Burning but another fleet beneath your flag,
Netting no pearls for your strong tides of wine;
Life melts in your body's cup –
O drink to the dregs ...

JUNE

The Eel-fisher:
'She gathers wet strawberries down in Ballivor,
For so I was told by a man on the Boyne,
Who pushed his old raft through a crush of bulrushes
And laughed when I told him I loved her.

'Come, Playboy, now this is a day for Ballivor;
I'll go there and leave you alone with your hounds –
While young squirrels dive here among the dark branches
And the Boyne is alive with blue salmon.'

The Fox-catcher:
'Then, lover, O why should you go to Ballivor
To stain your proud lips with a strawberry kiss?
If she cools her red mouth with the waves of the river
May the Boyne bring you that berry!'

ABOVE

A lone grey heron is flying, flying
    Home to her nest,
And over the rush-blown waters
    Burning in the west,
Where an orange moon is lying
    Softly on soft air,
As the dusk comes lounging after
    Sleepy care.

Ah, now that heron is slowly, slowly
    Plying her wing,
But soon she'll droop to the rushes
    Where the winds swing;
She'll stand in the pools and coldly
    Dream on the sly,
With her wild eyes watching the fishes,
    As stars watch you from on high.

THE MOUNTAINY YEW

As I passed through the dews of West Munster
I pulled the red fruit of the yew,
And the heel of my fist held riches
That even the birds hardly knew;
I driving my white drift of asses –
Ah, never such grandeur was seen,
In the deeps of that country morning,
Since the women of Beare grew lean.

Not many miles after in Connacht
The sun slipped away from the birds,
And I buried that Munster yew berry
In true soil untrodden by herds;
But its growth in the night-time had opened
A green hand of hush on my house,
I outgrew the sun on my windows
And hid Nephin Beg in its boughs

That yew gave me music and shelter
And the food that flew down to its fruits,
Until age had knuckled its branches
And rocks took sap from its roots;
It was then that I hewed from its timbers
Bright floors level under the shoe;
But these, with the keeves and three cradles,
Have only laths left of the yew;

Just boards for the fire or for turning
To sweet pipes, as cool on the tongue
As honey pulled newly in June time –
To suckle while evenings are young;
But four of those boards in a coffin
Will crumble my white bones to

The quiet of dew in West Munster,
The smell of red fruit from a yew!

RUINS

Cold, cold are the low fields,
    And rain pools lie
Gaping after that bleak sun,
    Sunk in a rainy sky;
While shivering like an old crane,
    I dream of the hushful breasts,
When crows flap home through the shadows
    To slim boughs heavy with nests.

My love, it is well for the badger,
    Warm in his furzy den –
For the fish of a sedgy river
    Untroubled by men;
It is well for the summer-bound cuckoo,
    Whose voice isn't wandering where
Far voices were toned at a hearthstone
    Which starving hills strip bare –

Could I lift up a door on that threshold
    And the sills from this grassy floor,
I would gather some rods for the thatching
    And the folk as before;
With tobacco stacked over a dresser,
    And surely some blue willow ware
Once stolen from bold Marco Polo
    When hookers blew everywhere.

ISLAND BLOOD

If I could spare good money,
 I would spread a sail and ride
Towards lakes that glow like honey
 In a bloom of country-side –
While island blood is restless
 For the whin-lit country-side.

Just now the curlews hover
 By each wave-wet river isle,
And evening wets the clover
 And loud crows crowd Renvyle –
But cool woods gather music
 From the clovers of Renvyle.

Soon dark men from the glenside
 And bare-limbed girls with creels
Shall wade along the ebb-tide
 And rake the sand for eels –
With moonlight on the bare strand
 They'll prong the bright sand-eels.

O could I hear their talking
 As they hod home through the dark;
Could I but hear their walking
 Rise pheasant, fox, or lark,
My shoes would wake the mountain
 As the air wakes to the lark.

But it's down a ship of thin trees
 I hod through this bitter foam,
With green wine from the Indies
 To whet wild lips in Rome –
Ah, soon I'll whet lips sweeter
 Than a cardinal's in Rome.

And soon I'll net that lover
    In the clovers of Renvyle,
Though wild as the silver flashing
    From nets by the bilberry isle –
That star of a hundred islands
    I'll set on my river isle.

THE BROKEN TRYST

A full red moon at the rim of the earth,
    And the stars in the purple air;
The salleys are swaying over the pond
    And three boys sit fishing there.

Into the sedges a waterhen flies,
    As slowly the twilight and evening pass;
A fishing rod bends, and the boys arise
    To look at a dying perch in the grass.

But now they are going, one by one,
    And the last of all he carries the prize,
While here by the salleys I wait alone –
    And only the shadows look into my eyes ...

from
The Dark Breed
(London, Macmillan, 1927)

THE DARK BREED

With those bawneen men I'm one,
    In the grey dusk-fall,
Watching the Galway land
    Sink down in distress –
With dark men, talking of grass,
    By a loose stone wall,
In murmurs drifting and drifting
    To loneliness.

Over this loneliness.
    Wild riders gather their fill
Of talking on beasts and on fields
    Too lean for a plough,
Until, more grey than the grey air,
    Song drips from a still,
Through poteen, reeling the dancing –
    Ebbing the grief now!

Just, bred from the cold lean rock,
    Those fellows have grown;
And only in that grey fire
    Their lonely days pass
To dreams of far clovers
    And cream-gathering heifers, alone
Under the hazels of moon-lighters,
    Clearing the grass.

Again in the darkness,
    Dull knives we may secretly grease,
And talk of blown horns on clovers
    Where graziers have lain;
But there rolls the mist,
    With sails pulling wind from the seas –

No bullion can brighten that mist,
  O brood of lost Spain.

So we, with the last dark men,
  Left on the rock grass,
May brazen grey loneliness
  Over a poteen still
Or crowd on the bare chapel floor
  Hearing late Mass,
To loosen that hunger
  Broken land never can fill.

HERESY

What peace have I in holy bonds,
From chiselled holiness on stone,
Where croziers, flowering in white bronze,
And fiery minds have finely shown
The grace of God in metal?

So when the quiet shoes my feet
And this hill-pool has cupped the moon,
I'll lie with God and slowly beat
My lonely thought into a tune,
That we may chant together.

Unravelling no gilded prayer,
I'll praise the Scribe, whose burning lines,
On that pure vellum of blue air,
Shoot crimson stars through golden signs
Around the flaming spiral;

And safe beneath those fiery snakes,
His breviary of sleep I'll tell,
Until the shining morning shakes
This calm hill to a laughing bell
And leads the day with singing.

THE FAIR OF MAAM

Pursuing my love's wild heart
   From rumours through many a fair,
I roved under miles of pinewood
   Through days of blue dusk air;
To meet the fair day at Maam
   To gather sly rumours of her,
I took the pinewoods for my bed
   And slept until dawn made a stir.

The stir of heifers and young bulls
   Had hoofed soil under the pine,
Through fresh woods smelling of cattle,
   Through dawn airs, moistured and fine;
And I, at a heel of soft herds,
   Stepped from the heavy air
To a green square, gabled with pinewoods –
   The fair-green of Maam fair.

All day in the slapping of bargains
   I sought for word of my love;
And what had crowded my hearing,
   But loud strokes herding each drove,
Horns buckling by bullocks unnozzled;
   Strong words of praise or blame
Were heard from sly ass dealers –
   But never my love's name!

And evening crowded the pinewoods
   When all but my love were seen;
For hearing a reel of fife music
   Rise on the loose fair-green,
Girls hurried from under green timbers
   To dancers grown lively in ale,

To matchmakers, by the bone-fire,
  That welded the female to male.

Then leaving the fair-green of Maam
  The ballad-men sang my love
Until the glens whispered her name
  That hill voices whispered above;
The pools of sunrise had not wet her,
  So I crept where the moonlight creeps
To look on the unknown mountains
  And plunder their blue deeps.

I've lost her, O loved one, O strange one,
  O hunger none other can ease;
Crossroads of the Black Bull deceived me,
  Courtyards by the eastern seas;
Grown peevish, I'm beggared in Maam,
  Its woods are all gone and its fair
Is a memory left to the old men
  Who tether a few goats there.

THE ISLAND DEAD OF INCHIGOILL

On the blue road through Moytura
   I heard from cairns overthrown
Stone cutters ringing the Gospels
   On crosses of fiery stone,
For saints grown quiet in granite
   Carven with sunless hoods,
While men wielded flighty axes
   That buried sharp light in woods.

Come, woodmen, O sweet strings quicken
   On harps strange women made
So flawlessly from green salleys,
   That shadowed a heron's wade;
These murmur still of rich waters,
   Lost woods and the healing of sleep
From grasses in arable holdings,
   From stills making music leap!

Wild light from crown and red crozier
   Is quenched now in holy Cong;
No king takes sleep from grey poteen,
   And leaner than a church song
The bishop in pure black ashes
   Lies in a place of wakes –
Their white pipes strewn on the tombstones
   Of drownings in Galway lakes.

So, woodmen, tune up! and stone cutters
   You quicken your silvern notes,
Although not one yellow coffin
   Is due for the funeral boats;
We've lost all our beautiful faces,
   Moytura has taken its fill,

Those acres of dark lake water
Bore harvest for Inchigoill.

A TINKER'S WOMAN

I'll throw no sorrowful hair at her –
    No tears for you, MacDara
For pride of beauty takes no slur
    When fierce of limb, MacDara;
You thought my body's shine grew dusk
Beside that girl you took at Lusk –
Yet who but a fool would pluck the husk
    And leave the fruit to wither.

You now forget when from the gorse
    I saw you swim sea water,
Stark naked I flashed on a tinker's horse
    Down to the morning water
And into green seas I took my ride
Barebacked, horse-swimming I reached your side,
Then who but a fool would rob the tide
    And throw away the salmon.

Ah, now I know you wrongly thought
    You loved me then, MacDara,
While peeled to the waist for me you fought
    Some mountainy fellow, MacDara,
For there on wet grass and stript to my teeth
I seemed as a sword of light at your feet –
Yet who but a fool would keep the sheath
    And leave the sword unhandled.

So now I'll throw no curse before
    Your lean ways with young women,
For I'm too ripe in the old sun's lore
    To envy slips of women;
Then keep the girlish slip who went
To whet your taste, last night in my tent,

For who but a fool would look for scent
  Along a budless bramble.

Red Barbara

Along the airy tops of morning
　　I scaled a wandering mile;
And coming on a tremble of water
　　Slyly I watched awhile
Your nimble fingers building there –
　　Pile on sunny pile –
The silken architecture
　　Of your hair.

But since against your shining beauty,
　　My shadow stains the sun
Along the ways you set me awander;
　　And now I drift upon
The cold shore of each gleaming crowd –
　　Crowds I proudly shun,
To follow darkness for a
　　Fiery cloud.

Until upon the airy windings
　　Each morning finds me near
Your sunhouse, shining with soft women,
　　And with your voice I hear
Strings, laughing in a river of sound –
　　Strings, the old crones fear,
That ghostly fingers weave on
　　Moonlit ground.

Yet Barbara your shining body
　　Storms from the cold clear air;
Your eagle blood still leads the horse herd
　　Over the horse-dealers' fair;
And now for men of lost desire,
　　Head of the evil hair,

Arise and shatter twilight
  With your fire.

ALL SOULS' EVE

The grey air was thinning
  Over the red lake,
Shading pale herons
  Scarcely awake;
Until on still grasses,
  On shores of cold dew,
The bright ring of sunset
  More brightly grew.

Then mooring my curragh
  In yew trees awhile,
I crushed through the wet dusk
  Of a deep isle;
And cleaving boughs over
  One moonless place,
I stood in the pale light
  Of a pale face.

That face it moved gently
  As dew on the air;
'O come,' she said softly,
  Her eyes told me where;
Her words they grew dreamy,
  Her voice gave no fear –
The voice of my true love
  Dead for a year!

I loosened my curragh
  From a yew bough,
Surrounded by music –
  I scarcely hear now
Away on grey waters,
  Away on the lake,

And half of my senses
  Barely awake.

POACHERS

Although each Galway wood
   Has been our bed
Of marriage this many a year,
   Here come let us spread
Rushes again for love,
   Housing from eyes outside,
Where netting the sea's live glitter
   Those salmon poachers hide.

Bright love, from the waters of dew
   I have moved to this night
Wilder in sport than poachers –
   Whose draw-nets gathering light
Into a shivering pile,
   Heap treasures on the shore –
While rushes net you, my treasure,
   Isled on my rush floor.

Then what thin sign of a moon
   Curled in the leap
Of sea-ripened salmon,
   Shall tempt me out to reap
That silver flowing far over
   Those shoals in the warm deep?
While we in a breathless dark
   Grow empty of sleep?

So here as a poacher I'll gather
   Your body's white gleam;
For too soon rushes wither
   And in a cold dream
Now cuckoos stir and the close night
   On our window has gone;

O, quickly rise up, my bright love,
   And quench the dawn!

THE GHOST

Ah, Auina Costello,
   Although I have known
The soft shores of heaven
   And hell's cold stone,
Earth-tainted I mingle
   With airs we knew
And break in blue trembles
   Of night, on you.

In these fruit-tree spaces,
   Wet airs cry to-night,
Cries stripping salt branches
   Smelt in moonlight,
Of windy fresh leavings
   From every harsh tree –
Braced with salt tastings
   Of a heard sea.

These boughs drop their voices;
   Now this still place,
O, Auina Costello,
   And your lone face
Refashions the lost earth
   My song once knew,
Drenched in a soft West,
   Illumed by you.

Still you keep our trysting,
   Knowing how I
Am now in a pale wave
   Of island sky;
Here stript to my dreamings,
   Beyond death I am

The fierce breath of Tauris,
   The hoof lust of Ram!

Hush, woman; no murmur,
   Though moonlight endows,
Yet stints, windy silver
   On black fruit-boughs;
No murmur, no sorrow,
   While Time ebbing by,
Flickers false moon-dials
   With a swift sky.

LAKE DWELLERS

Hush, wordy one, hush!
    No sound, no stir,
Not a bulrush
    Sways on the water;
Not a wind haws
On pools, where dawn was
    Plunged by an otter.

For mating time, I
    Stocked in dull water
Boughs from the wild sky;
    Stapling our dwelling,
With raw lime and larch –
Over that lake marsh,
    Scared to the lapwing.

So, drowsy head, rest
    Deep in those feathers –
Piled from some high nest
    Of moulting wild geese –
Resting the bright head,
Shyly on our bed,
    Quilted with peace.

While to those isles, grown
    Heavy with dew-shine,
Thin woods have shown,
    In broken dusklight,
The sword light of kerns,
Float as twin herns,
    Fording the swift night.

But shining love, sleep
    Opens frail worlds –

The foolish fish leap
    Through stars by our threshold
Breaking on curds
Of dew-light, where shore birds,
    Nod in the cold.

Ah, soon you shall sink
    Through charms of slumber;
The rush candles wink,
    Yet no shadow creeps;
No sound, no stir –
The gentle lake dweller
    Sleeps ...

THE LITTLE CLAN

Over their edge of earth
    They wearily tread,
Leaving the stone-grey dew –
    The hungry grass;
Most proud in their own defeat,
    These last men pass
This labouring grass that bears them
    Little bread.

Too full their spring tide flowed,
    And ebbing then
Has left each hooker deep
    Within salt grass;
All ebbs, yet lives in their song;
    Song shall not pass
With these most desperate,
    Most noble men!

Then, comfort your own sorrow;
    Time has heard
One groping singer hold
    A burning face;
You mourn no living Troy,
    Then mourn no less
The living glory of
    Each Gaelic word!

from
Arable Holdings
(Dublin, The Cuala Press, 1933)

GRACE BEFORE BEER

For what this house affords us,
Come, praise the brewer most –
Who caught into a bottle
The barley's gentle ghost –
Until our parching throttles
In silence we employ –
Like geese that drink a mouthful,
Then stretch their necks in joy!

FATHER AND SON

Only last week, walking the hushed fields
Of our most lovely Meath, now thinned by November,
I came to where the road from Laracor leads
To the Boyne river – that seemed more lake than river,
Stretched in uneasy light and stript of reeds.

And walking longside an old weir
Of my people's, where nothing stirs – only the shadowed
Leaden flight of a heron up the lean air –
I went unmanly with grief, knowing how my father,
Happy though captive in years, walked last with me there.

Yes, happy in Meath with me for a day
He walked, taking stock of herds hid in their own breathing;
And naming colts, gusty as wind, once steered by his hand
Lightnings winked in the eyes that were half shy in greeting
Old friends – the wild blades, when he gallivanted the land.

For that proud, wayward man now my heart breaks –
Breaks for that man whose mind was a secret eyrie,
Whose kind hand was sole signet of his race,
Who curbed me, scorned my green ways, yet increasingly loved me
Till Death drew its grey blind down his face.

And yet I am pleased that even my reckless ways
Are living shades of his rich calms and passions -
Witnesses for him and for those faint namesakes
With whom now he is one, under yew branches,
Yes, one in a graven silence no bird breaks.

O, You Among Women

When pails empty the last brightness
Of the well, at twilight-time,
And you are there among women –
O, mouth of silence,
Will you come with me, when I sign,
To the far green wood, that fences
A lake inlaid with light?

To be there, O, lost in each other,
While day melts in airy water,
And the drake-headed pike – a shade
In the waves' pale stir!
For love is there, under the breath,
As a coy star is there in the quiet
Of the wood's blue eye.

To My Blackthorn Stick

When sap ebbed low and your green days were over –
Hedging a gap to rugged land,
Bare skinned and straight you were; and there I broke you
To champion my right hand.

Well shod in bronze and lithe with hillside breeding,
Yet, like a snarl, you dogged my side,
Mailed in your tridents and flaunting out the fierceness
That bristled through your hide.

So armed as one, have we not shared each journey
On noiseless path or road of stone;
O exiled brother of the flowering sloe tree,
Your past ways are my own.

Lonesome, like me, and song-bred on Mount Nephin,
You, also, found that in your might
You broke in bloom before the time of leafing
And shocked a world with light.

But you grew shy,– eyed through by glowering twilights –
Sharing the still of night's grey brew,
Secret and shy, while things unseen were sighing
Their grass tunes under you.

Manured with earth's own sweat you stretched in saplings;
Seasoned, you cored your fruit with stone;
Then stript in fight, your strength came out of wrestling
All winds by winter blown.

I took that strength; my axe blow was your trumpet,
You rose from earth, god-cleaned and strong;
And here, as in green days you were the perch,
You're now the prop of song.

THE OLD JOCKEY

His last days linger in that low attic
That barely lets out the night,
With its gabled window on Knackers' Alley,
Just hoodwinking the light.

He comes and goes by that gabled window
And then on the window-pane
He leans, as thin as a bottled shadow –
A look and he's gone again:

Eyeing, maybe, some fine fish-women
In the best shawls of the Coombe
Or, maybe, the knife-grinder plying his treadle,
A run of sparks from his thumb!

But, O you should see him gazing, gazing,
When solemnly out on the road
The horse-drays pass overladen with grasses,
Each driver lost in his load;

Gazing until they return; and suddenly,
As galloping by they race,
From his pale eyes, like glass breaking,
Light leaps on his face.

CRADLE SONG

Out in the dark something complains,
Is it the wild dove's purr?
And there a thing creeps, is it the rain
Eavesdropping near our door?
Then sleep, sleep, my darling –
Sleep until the bow-legged crows
Walk the fields of barley.

May nothing nose the gentle birds,
Abroad in the crawl of night,
Nor the cock, with wings upon his spurs,
Until the peep of light;
Then sleep to my long rocking;
Sleep as the little winds that sleep
All safely in God's pocket –
    Yes, safely in God's pocket,
    Sleep, my darling.

THE WOMAN OF THE RED-HAIRED MAN

At home last year soft airs were growing
From Candlemas to Lammas night;
Down my stone fields high dew was cropping
On edges of the twilight;
And summer climbed, when she who was wedded
Came to me and said: "With me you'll find
Bee's comb and black ale in a meadow
That's mowed to brightness by the wind."

O secret love, wild limb of beauty
Toppling with summers bloused in silk;
Yes, secret love, would that your bosom
By me grew full of milk –
Then as a goldsmith working with sunlight,
In isles of humming or some dark town,
Time could bring to us a sovereign wonder
With my harp under your black crown!

But now while I lie down in bracken
And foxes bark above my bed,
As married maid to red O'Meara
Your head lies by his head;
With black eyelashes, flags of mourning,
You mark the graves where love is laid;
O dreamy head, by you I'm broken
To run hare-brained and passion-flayed!

With salt I'm cursed, by church I'm banished
Beyond your parish mearing stones;
This Lent I've left black fast and ashes
With parish holy bones;
Salt days at table, nights without marriage
Leave milkless paps in your female clan –

But after Easter who'll ease your passion,
O woman of the red-haired man?

PADRAIC O'CONAIRE – GAELIC STORY-TELLER
(Died in the Fall of 1928)

They've paid the last respects in sad tobacco
And silent is this wakehouse in its haze;
They've paid the last respects; and now their whiskey
Flings laughing words on mouths of prayer and praise;
And so young couples huddle by the gables,
O let them grope home through the hedgy night –
Alone I'll mourn my old friend, while the cold dawn
Thins out the holy candlelight.

Respects are paid to one loved by the people:
Ah, was he not – among our mighty poor –
The sudden wealth cast on those pools of darkness,
Those bearing just, a star's faint signature;
And so he was to me, close friend, near brother,
Dear Padraic of the wide and sea-cold eyes –
So loveable, so courteous and noble,
The very West was in his soft replies.

They'll miss his heavy stick and stride in Wicklow –
His story-talking down Winetavern Street,
Where old men sitting in the wizen daylight
Have kept an edge upon his gentle wit;
While women on the grassy streets of Galway,
Who hearken for his passing – but in vain,
Shall hardly tell his step as shadows vanish
Through archways of forgotten Spain.

Ah, they'll say: Padraic's gone again exploring;
But now down glens of brightness, O he'll find
An alehouse overflowing with wise Gaelic
That's braced in vigour by the bardic mind,
And there his thoughts shall find their own forefathers –
In minds to whom our heights of race belong,

In crafty men, who ribbed a ship or turned
The secret joinery of song.

Alas, death mars the parchment of his forehead;
And yet for him, I know, the earth is mild –
The windy fidgets of September grasses
Can never tease a mind that loved the wild;
So drink his peace – this grey juice of the barley
Runs with a light that ever pleased the eye –
While old flames nod and gossip on the hearthstone
And only the young winds cry.

MEATH MEN

When soft grass gives the udders comeliness,
Before late milking-time in Meath and Carlow,
Come, Macnamara, in whiskey let us bless
The pastured royalties of Tara.

This is our land; and here no summer mocks
The stony crops we've known in Aran Islands,
Where seas break silence and strip the yellow rocks
Of rich top-dressing for lean highlands.

What of those lips, where Connemara sups
The poteen Connacht drips from yeast and barley,
While, Macnamara, we crown our royal cups
With whiskey from the wheats of Tara.

Here, drowned within their dewy deeps of June,
The fields, for graziers, gather evening silver;
And while each isle becomes a bush in tune,
The Boyne flows into airy stillness.

Yet by the weirs, that shiver with dark eels,
Dusk breaks in leaps of light; and salmon-snarers
Are nightly sharing fish in salley creels
That merely seem a dream to Clare-men.

Now in this halfway house my song is set,
So shut your mouth and let me kiss the barmaid;
For Brinsley Macnamara, you dare not forget
The poets and their privileges in Tara.

A Poor Girl

Had I goats, with golden eyes dreamy on brambles,
Or those cropping salt on Blacksod,
I'd now know the lad, who stepped to the goat fair,
Fresh from the woods of God!

I'd now know the lad, before whose sharp beauty
Men gasped and for whose bed
Young women were moved – with hearts of money
And limbs as lean as thread.

Ah, what could they give but yields of tillage;
It's love he'd get from me –
Not houses propped in waves of ploughing;
My house – the bend of a tree!

Maybe that's why, on that mountainy fair-green,
He drank with a women or two,
And never looked once, as I, with the goat herds
Shrank in a drift of dew.

Last night by a loose wall, mortared with moonlight,
I dreamt of my mind's desire,
But I saw myself, like an old crane, gazing
Over a pool of fire!

EXHORTATION

Come let us praise the glorious craft of these
Who knotting God's thought in metal, ink or rock
Make to a lasting dream what came as a breeze
From isles, where the saints in wind-preened garlic caught,
Through beehive dwellings, God's sweetness and
from that stock
Turned a pale honey to our cells of thought.

Through them men are, no more, as a midnight wood
Nudged by lewd winds, nor the heart a deep dark nest
Where claws and bearded eyes search through the blood,
Souring the honey hived for other minds;
For now, O God be praised, in the pure cold West
These claws and eyes are caged in chaste designs.

So, for all book-shrines, caging the serpent tribe
Clasped in their own enamels and silvered glues,
Come praise the whitesmith, yes and praise the scribe,
Whose airy quills light on a pastured skin
Netting the heavens into the selfsame hues
That manacle with rainbows the glooms of sin.

Bestowers of jewels and food, why stint your praise?
You with the grace to give, come forth and allot
Wicklow's raw gold for smith-work and flocks to raise
Books without censors; so shall our island be
A shrine of living mightiness and not
An Easter Island in the western sea.

from
The Gap of Brightness
(London, Macmillan, 1940)

THE BOYNE WALK
(To R .M. Smyllie)

'What's all this rich land,' said I to the Meath man,
'Just mirrors bedazzled with blazing air!'
And like flies on mirrors my parched thoughts ran
As we walked, half-hidden, through where the reeds stand
Between the Boyne and its green canal;
And sweltering I kept to the pace he planned,
Yet he wouldn't even wait in the reeds
To watch a red perch, like a Japanese hand,
Grope in the sun-shot water and weeds –
He merely called back: 'O, go be damned!'

With break-neck looks at the withered end
Of a stupefied town, I paced his heel
By moat, dead wall and under an arch
That was all of a crouch with the weight of years;
But where the road led I'd have seen – were I wise –
From one running look in the dark of his eyes:
For each seemed the bright astrological plan
Of a new Don Quixote and his man
Again on campaign; but lacking their steeds,
I'd sooner have seen a flick of grey ears
Or a blue lackadaisical eye in the reeds
To lead to a smoky bare back; then, cheers!
We'd have ridden our road as the Kings of Meath.

We walked, as became two kings outcast
From plains walled in by a grass-raising lord,
Whose saint is the Joker, whose hope is the Past –
What victuals for bards could that lad afford?
O, none! So off went his dust from our boots,
But his dust that day was of buttercup gold
From a slope, with a sight that was, man alive, grand:
Just two servant girls spreading blue clothes

On grass too deep for a crow to land;
And though they waved to us we kept on our track,
And though to the bank their own clothes soon toppled
We sweltered along – while my thoughts floated back
Through shy beauty's bathing-pool, like an old bottle!

Heat trembled in halos on grass and on cattle
And each rock blazed like a drunken face;
So I cried to the man of the speedy wattle
'In the name of Lot's wife will you wait a space?
For Adam's red apple hops dry in my throttle,'
And yet instead of easing the pace,
I saw on the broad blackboard of his back
His muscles made signs of a far greater chase,
Until as I tried to keep up on his track
Each pore of my skin became a hot spring
And every bone swam in a blister of pains
While all my bent body seemed as an old crane's
Lost in a great overcoat of wings.

Soon out from my sight off went the big Meath man
Dodging the reeds of his nine-mile road.
So I lolled, as a bard bereft of his daemon
Or a Moses, awaiting a light-burdened cloud;
But heaven lay low all naked and brazen
Within the mad calm on that desert of green,
Where nothing, not even the water, is lean,
Where the orderly touches of Thought aren't seen –
And yet not a wild thought sang in my noddle;
Ah, how could it sing, while speed bit each heel,
While heat tugged a tight noose into my throttle
And while, on my spine, the hung head went nodding
As on it fierce light picked with a black bill.

Then where in soft Meath can one find ease?
When the sun, like a scarecrow, stands in those meadows

Guarding their glory, not even the breeze,
That ghostly rogue, can crop a shadow;
When even I asked for 'A drink, if you please,'
A woman, as proud as a motherly sow,
Hoked out of my way and hid where a larch
Leant like a derrick across an old barge
Stocked in the reeds; and so I went parched!
Ah, but soon down the Boyne, there O the surprise
From a leaping fish – that silver flicker –
Was nothing compared to what hit my eyes:
An innocent house, marked 'Licensed for Liquor!'

Could anyone treat me to brighter green meadows
Than the Meath man who finished his thirsty plan when
Between every swig he mooned through those windows?
And yet, on my oath, it was easier then
To coop a mountainy cloud in a henhouse
Than to group the Meath light into lines for my pen;
And still I must bless him since beauty was caught
In ears that were drumming, in eyes all sweat,
In nostrils slimmed by indrawn breath;
For I made, as we lay in the grass by that road
This poem – a gem from the head of a toad;
So here, will you take it – hall-marked by a day
Over the hills and far away?

SONG FOR THE CLATTER-BONES

God rest that Jewy woman,
Queen Jezebel, the bitch
Who peeled the clothes from her shoulder-bones
Down to her spent teats
As she stretched out of the window
Among the geraniums, where
She chaffed and laughed like one half daft
Titivating her painted hair –

King Jehu he drove to her,
She tipped him a fancy beck,
But he from his knacky side-car spoke,
'Who'll break that dewlapped neck?'
And so she was thrown from the window;
Like Lucifer she fell
Beneath the feet of the horses and they beat
The light out of Jezebel.

That corpse wasn't planted in clover;
Ah, nothing of her was found
Save those grey bones that Hare-foot Mike
Gave me for their lovely sound;
And as once her dancing body
Made star-lit princes sweat,
So I'll just clack: though her ghost lacks a back
There's music in the old bones yet.

CHINESE WINTER

From these bare trees
The stick of last year's nests
Print sad characters against the moon;
While wind-blown moonlight,
Stripping fields to silver,
Scrawls December on each frozen pool.

Light washed on each tree
Roots it in black shadow,
As last year's love now roots me in black night;
And where love danced,
Footprints of fiery moments
Flash out memorials in silent ice.

THE GAP OF BRIGHTNESS

Although you smelt of tillage,
Great hostings and the herds
That stretched in a hill's green hammock,
Were tented in your woods;
And borne on those heroics
I found their forts up here,
All bannered with lark-music –
And not a hero near!

Where are the horn-winged griffins –
The elk and eagle clan,
That climbed, where only gold light
And living rivers ran?
And their sun-rutted fierceness
Has it too ebbed from here –
With eagles and with, even,
The breezy-footed deer?

With these, your dream-battalions
Just perished when clear day
Camped on this gap of brightness –
Searching each face of clay,
And hailing, as radiant allies,
Only poets whose mirth
Shortened the four roads, knotted
Over this parcelled earth.

These poets are captains; ale-boughs, their banners –
Through them brave music flows
From those hedge schools, where no song withered
Nor faltered when Owen Roe's
Lightheaded and footless music
Tricked there, with Cathal Bwee's

That had the knack of throwing
A bright skin over grief.

There Carolan's laugh was a tinkle of glasses;
There his last finger-tap
Drew from the wood the chirping chill music
Of mornings while Raftery sat
Stroking a sad-faced fiddle
To woo those home-spun lines
That stitched the fine airs of heaven
In a shift for young Miss Hynes.

Hedge names in bard-craft! Green isles that harbour
Wild seas of staggering light!
Ah, these brighten wreckage, as Red MacNamara
In Hamburg made exile bright,
When – through the gabled shadows
Scaffolded by spar and mast –
His song poured blessing over
Hills holy with the past.

Let these hills cease as skylines
On greater peaks we'll gaze –
Peaks, horned with frozen brightness
Isled in long drifts of haze –
Gaze from those trembling silvers
Where eagled minds have stood
As stars by the sun begotten,
As twins to the eagle brood.

Yes, strong men smelt of tillage,
And kings were bred from herds –
These never raised as banner
The bladder of your words
Nor called the carrion crow down
To pick the mind until

The eye's light is mere slobber
Upon a stone-wiped bill.

STAR-GAZERS

From the grey east,
Through night, noon and the morning,
Into the west
They followed a blue flame;
Like kingfisher's wings
It went as it was leading
These, the wise kings
From lands without a name.

Whitely it stood
Above a moulding townland,
And over the wooden
Green dwellings of the poor,
Till with the dewfall
It quietly slid down and
Shone, as a jewel,
On the brow of a door.

There, with no din,
On floorings of cool rushes,
The wise kings went in –
And from an ingle bed
A young woman smiled,
As proudly in her blushes
She breasted a child,
And on a dream He fed.

Down on the floor
These served Him on the knee, when
Each gave him their store's
Untouchable delights –
Gemmed like a seaboard
And scents preserved from Eden –

Gifts the cold sword
Brought through Arabian nights.

So they arose
But doing so they opened –
Out of a doze –
His eyes from other worlds:
Then O His look held each mind,
Till each saw, through deep darkness,
Upon Hell's dead wind,
The white flag was unfurled!

From the green west,
As out of an aurora,
Into the east
These wise kings picked their way;
Close as God's gossips
They went; and now our skylines
Are hailstoned with stars
That tell – ah, who can say?

AT FLOCK MASS

I only knew her as a spouse
Whose match with me enlarged my herd;
– A wife well mated to the house,
So mild in movement, soft in word,
That who would heed her in the room
At hearth or needle, bread or broom?

But yesterday at Galway sports,
In a drinking-tent, a man told me
Of beauties handled in Spanish ports;
'Yet cross-eyed would they seem,' said he,
'Near one outside, whose look cowed mine
And she demurely sipping wine.

Have you not seen her, O, her mouth:
A bud, maybe – the flower's hint;
Unfathomed wells from nights of drought
Have filled her eyes; and what a dint
Between each snowy breast, each limb –
As if a neat breeze moulded them.'

And so I listened till he said,
'O there she is!' Then, on my life,
I thought the drink had turned his head
To throw such beauty on my wife!
But there, by hell, I see it's true –
Just look at her tip to her pew!

She genuflects; and our new priest
Looks – only to falter in the Mass;
Even the alter boy has ceased
And his responses, now alas,
Are not 'amen' – but towards the door
He seems to sigh: *a stoir, a stoir.*

AUCTION!
(*To Lynn Doyle*)

Listen, you graziers, men of stealth,
Gentlemen jobbers, heavy in dung;
I've under this hammer; miles of green wealth,
An eel-run slipped from the river's tongue,
A house of ghosts and that among
Gardens where even the Spring is old;
So gather around, the sale is on
And nods and winks spell out in gold
Going, going, gone.

Who bids for that stone wall and gate?
Come, gentlemen, their worth is known
To you who stared against their weight
And stared so long that O you've grown,
With eyes of hunger, hard as stone;
Now they'll no more hang out the sun
Nor gaol the best of grass that's grown;
These walls are yours, their day is done,
Going, going, gone.

And there's the timber you have cashed,
Weighed and measured in a squint;
Fatherly trees that from a past
Of windy traffic made a mint
Of golden rings for their heart's content –
They'll make the teeth of sawmills water;
So better your bids; and here's a hint,
The Boyne will be your gentle carter,
Going, going, gone.

Well, boys alive, and who'd desire
Keener bidding, neater fight;
Even the skin-flint kindles fire,

Even the tight-lipped purses bite
At fields, that seemed one green delight
To slyly dream upon in pubs –
When the last drinks were out of sight;
So easy on, men, spare my lugs,
Going, going, gone.

Now, I'll knock down to this fine throng
The spacious park – once great and grand –
That Higgins mortgaged for a song;
For even had old Euclid planned
Its blue prints with his gilded hand,
See there before you: grace gone wild
And beauty run to earth, a land
Of gentleness that's all shop-soiled,
Going, going, gone.

But that's the best soil cropped for coin;
Good money there like mushrooms creep
Out of pastures where the Boyne
Drains the heavy fields of sleep;
Why, even look, the frail winds heap
Fierce silver on the sally hedge
And sods are fortunes going cheap –
Enough to put your teeth on edge:
Going, going, gone.

So the last field falls to a nod,
Falls from a red indentured deed
To you whose hearts throb on the sod,
Beef-belted, pea-eyed men of Meath:
You've got the lot by nothing said,
Indeed, you speak that common tongue
Of silence spoken by the dead –
For in close darkness all is one,
Going, going, gone.

Jobbers in land! And so you pass
The graces by and only yawn;
Ah, what to you this genteel grass,
This willowed, bronzed, umbrellaed lawn
As calm as when Palm Sunday shone
Through aisles of elm where Stella drove
With Doctor Swift to Evensong,
While crows in each black chapter strove;
Going, going, gone.

These things are now not worth a curse –
Faint patterns from a willow plate;
Look at the house! What could be worse
Than that old peacock roost of late?
Its rooky stair sways at your weight
To rooms of yellow, blue and pink
Where feather-brainlings titivate
And then cold shoulder those they think
Going, going, gone.

Well, God be with the days of power –
Those ending with the crinoline,
When strength shone like an oak in flower
From minds that tied their time between
Old books, old wine and ladies seen
All musical in candlelight;
What then seemed bright by now seems mean
With things of wisdom, grace and might
Going, going, gone.

So the old home goes to the wall,
As goes its garden – so select –
With Time's green fingers slipping all;
The plum-trees keep the walls erect,
While ivies hold the stones intact;
And what seemed cribbed from Chinese schools,

That bridge-design! it, too, is wrecked
On a mosaic of midnight pools
Going, going, gone.

Then take for nothing that moss-house,
Once hedge-school to a gentle breed;
You'll see it, if the light allows,
Beyond the bee-hives hid beneath
Nettle-stock and chicken-weed;
So fare you well, well may you keep
These lands – my people's, yes, indeed –
For I've their dreams, in me they sleep,
Going, going, gone.

A Vision of Paradise Park
(After the Old Irish)

While waves were glazed with silence
Beneath a shadow's weight,
The still-house on Grass Island
Locked me in sleep last night;
And there, while souls from heaven
Came softly through my sleep,
One dressed in blue mist led me
Through fields of meal and mead.

From black lands we rowed over
The sacred river Boyne,
To where saints gamely sported;
There bagpipes cried with joy
When all God's walking beauties
Went by in nun-like robes
Or played on the grass and coolly
Slipped naked from their clothes.

But, O boys, what a glitter!
Some high-born angels lay
Preening their wings in the mirrored
Airs of Lady Day;
And glitters like them lit the hedgerows
When Lapp-faced cherubs went
Among the robins that echoed
The clinks of Peter's pence.

Nearby on a lake of music
I saw the Pascal sun
Dance when a hearty psalm tune
Was step-danced on a drum;
For all things moved in music –
Even the Tree of Good

And Evil sang like an anvil
As swords clashed round its fruit.

Cut stone rang with the Lord's name,
Brass eagles sang His glees,
The fingered leaves of laurel
Were folded with His peace;
Inks ran to hold His knowledge
While His own scribe adorned
Stags sheltering in a forest
Of their own legs and horns.

There lolled those wrinkled craftsmen,
Whose fingers once unlaced
The knots of thought in granite
From God's own hiding-place;
Ah, now they're all teetotallers,
Finding those Sunday streets
Of heavenly law and order
Policed by parish priests.

And away on the lake's lone islands,
Beside old beehive homes,
Calm waters hold the daylight
Till stars creep towards each door,
Where minds, tuned to a dewfall
And keyed to the voice of hills,
Please God in a stiller music
Than fingered wind or strings.

But these minds welded to glory
And those toned as one bell
In Paradise Park – all coldly
Sank from my eyes, until
One angled and arklike abbey
Through a blue mist shone, like a star

That lingered for the lost Magi,
Then quenched on a grey despair.

So alone I stared on the ghostly,
Frozen and foggy air;
Yes, coldly alone till slowly –
And naked as any snail –
A lost soul stood out on the white air;
And on his iceberg throne
I gazed and saw his dead face –
And that face was my own.

CHANGELING

Crazy for her and empty, weary,
Coatless and down at heel
I've trudged – since dusk showed up of a sudden
A young moon's screech of steel –
Over the hills hardened by black frost,
Into the needles of wind;
And yet I'm heady with sweetness for
She's always on my mind.

Were she bred from the silver roots of a well
Or from the green pulse of a tree,
I swear I'd still take her before the high altar
Of stars, to marry me;
And under a bush of blackthorn music,
We'd not leave the dew,
For she's too rare to taste the sun,
With all the common crew.

NIGHT FRENZY

Stretched out by the bed-stock of another!
My curse that I'm not my own;
For, yes, I am shaped to the veins of beauty –
Here soft, there round in the bone –
Well may the eye, the hand, admire me
And the far mouth that said:
'Ah, grief, that I can only bed you
In the wild thought of my head!'

So said my love, but I mind him saying:
'Since Maeve was housed in the West,
Though love goes down, its light strays over
The clear domes of your breast
And over your hip that turns to a crescent
After the sun has gone;
Then what of the dark and you my bright link
Between the dusk and dawn?'

O, look at me now, forced wife to another –
The graft for a stunted bough;
Yet, lover, your words still burnish my body
To such a light that now
Were only your far ear close to my thinking,
With me, I know, you'd pray
That as God's candles decay on the altar
So may his limbs decay.

Ah, what if I wish my bedded husband
The scarecrow's fate in a ditch,
Maybe with dreams of you I am souring –
A fruit grown over-rich!
Swoop down then, O love, lash up my body;
And in an eagle's nest,

Far from the cold tombstones of Irrus,
Your brood shall drain my breast.

O HAWKS CLAW-CLINCHED

O hawks, claw-clinched and bronze-plated
On your sun-splintered forts,
Brave winds be your perch to blaze on
The crows in our pastured slopes.

War-footed and braced by blood music –
Your poise is on perilous steps,
Remote from the grass-quiet humours
Of magpies in evening dress.

Ah, what of the spleens that grieve us,
Heart-breaks in our bitter town,
Our green air grows herbage for healing
Beneath the cool cheek of the moon.

Here willows with timber for harpers
Are lively; and yet our last bard
Lies under the grin of a gargoyle,
With potions once brewed by the dark.

Here beggars' eyes blaze with grey money,
When crystals are read in back rooms;
Here tinkers, through lean concertinas
Squeeze wind to a giggling tune.

But soon roots pale in foul cellars
Shall shoot forth leaf and unroof
The dark to the bright, marching heavens –
To those, your claw-clinched salute!

SILVER-POINT

Late last night the moon lay
With no move on wet, quiet yew;
No fool, through that hush of amber,
Stained acres of grey dew.

It was then when birds slept
And song dreamt under each wing,
That you eyed the quiet and gave us
Music from its pale sleeping.

As Time turned back in that sleep,
You, Seumas O'Sullivan,
Set all the gay ladies of Whaley
Raiding your Georgian lawn.

There Buck steered an Arabic stallion,
Necked like a scimitar,
Frantic through ladies who scattered
As bits of one burst star.

They're gone; yet each shining delight
Again tiptoes the dew –
Dusk-quiet, light-shy in June midnights
Of twilight – for you.

For you who quicken cold joy,
From a world scarcely awake
That gleams as the far sad glory
Of a frozen lake.

THE LITTLE CLAN

Over their edge of earth
    They wearily tread,
Leaving the stone-grey dew –
    The hungry grass;
Most proud in their own defeat,
    These last men pass
This labouring grass that bears them
    Little bread.

Too full their spring tide flowed,
    And ebbing then
Has left each hooker deep
    Within salt grass;
All ebbs, yet lives in their song;
    Song shall not pass
With these most desperate,
    Most noble men!

Then, comfort your own sorrow;
    Time has heard
One groping singer hold
    A burning face;
You mourn no living Troy,
    Then mourn no less
The living glory of
    Each Gaelic word!

THE PAST GENERATION

Cornered within a mind that from its dark berth
Sags like an old cobweb of wings and bones,
Yet clad in a fireside shadow – he sits inert,
A pensioned man of seventy years or so,
Nodding and leaning to feel the white dough
Ripening to bread upon a scorching hearth;
But once into the crust his thumb is spread –
With smells of yeast enlivening the air –
His eyes seem rich with black ale; he lifts the bread
As though his hands are full of prayer.

And while the cake cools within the window space
That pane of scowls glows like a holy place.

Browbeaten he stands there now scanning the mountain
That throws a long siege against the shadowy glass,
Blinding that spyhole, where light squeezed from the pincers
Of dusk and dark, like death, has creased his face –
Creased as his crushed eyes squint with strain of sinew,
Poor seedless skin, the jail of all his race,
The last thing human next the wind's dominion,
The one thing hostile to the mountain's peace:
– A peace unbroken save by a sudden fright
From creaking wild duck winged in headlong flight.

Against that huddled strength his hate is pitched;
And now he glowers at its roots of heath,
That squat their evil claws in this dark hour
Upon the thrown clay cabins of a street:
Homes like worn graves, tombstoned with the gables
That, shading our race once in the blazing years,
Sheltered those mothers, who breeding a stock of nobles
Raised them to grace with grey baptism of tears.

And yet that stock gave stark air a green delight:
Its young men, hardy, nimble of limb and wit
To shorten the road, inveigle a bird or bind
Proud necks to bridles and rough lands to wheat;
With girls of shy sweetness, superbly designed
From nape and hip to instep; while over each breast
Snuggled the lazy brightness of the West.

Now those delights are all gone; ah, look, old pry,
Where lightning struck, burnt bare that blossoming tree,
A black hand points indictment at the sky!

So he – last trembler from those heartscalding years –
Making this hour unearthly with the dead,
Ceases to spy on what the night has hid
And while each timid thing creeps into bed,
Clamping his door – more like a coffin lid –
He turns, he yawns and having locked the sashes
Calmly he rakes the fire, till deep in ashes
The hushed flame sleeps within its own red dream.

He's now in bed but there's not a sign he'll ease
The weight of the great sleep that's on his bones,
The weight that he has gathered with the years –
Too weary now he seems even to doze
And fearing death may oust him from those bones
'O holy God,' he sighs, he turns, he eyes
The bare-breast Virgin suckling Her Child
Printed in smoky gold above the bed.

And as he mouths Time's lullabies, his beads
Barely keep count of prayers in yawned retreats;
And so from floor and stool old shadows creep
With crickets ticking out the time of sleep.

THE VICTIM

Fiddle and fife play up!
Come, dancer, drain your cup;
Hurry, my marriage is due,
Are your eyes shot with sport?
Then come to the dark and court;
But, love, I cannot marry you ...
Last fair-day I was decked
Up in silks to the neck,
The fair stood hushed to let me by,
But there they made my match
To an old man with a crutch,
Whose green lands run to the sky.

Ah, what of his green coach,
His wine cups, his couch –
The pride of my poor kith and kin –
Beside your heart of wealth
And mouth so sweetly felt
This night beneath the creaky whin;
Without shawl, shift or shoe,
Crushed to sweetness by you,
I close my eyes in my first bloom;
Praying this tint of love
May for a lifetime prove
The fragrance in my living tomb.

Uncollected poems (1926–1939)
from *The Dublin Magazine*

THE MAN WHO SCARED THE PHOENIX

Last May eve in the Ox mountains,
Men lit a fire of whin
And blessed with flame the Ox mountains –
Where scant grasses begin.

Flame blessed scant grass and fresh cattle
Clamped through the fiery thorn,
Cleansing wild heifers with May-fire –
Their bull-calves unborn.

Bright steps, to merriest flute-tuners,
Had clipped the swift edge of flame;
Red embers were crushed by the ripe dancers,
Unknown to the love game!

But one man edged from the gay dancers –
That man in the lean grey clothes –
He made for home, with the May night-time
Struck pale where a dawn star rose.

Grown mean with the gnaw of land hunger,
He made for home by road
And over the gap of a crab orchard,
Against his cold abode.

Dull greys and greens of old silver
Into the dawn air came;
And there he saw in his crab orchard
A tuft of yellow flame.

He beat that flame and a sweet savour –
A tremble of burning spice –
Arose with the blows of his green hazel,
To a star still as ice!

He lashed that flame with his green hazel,
When fiercer than his desire
Out suddenly flashed a fierce bird from
That nest of ghostly fire.

It gathered each flame in its black feathers,
It took to the air, alas!
And left no trace where the fire nestled,
But wet orchard grass.

O grief! He scared from the Ox mountains
That light of luck when it came,
That bird with feathers sweet smelling
And bones nurtured with flame.

And now our fine men unmarrying
Pass to the American sea;
One deed has withered the Ox mountains,
And life withers in me.

A Shade from Limestone

While blood ran wild, for her he drew
   White yewan wood and stone;
And where the yewan wood was planed,
   The limestone married loam,
Rearing an airy house for her,
   With copings clearly shown,
Against the air from Galway,
   As cool tunes of stone.

Such graceful tones have rarely paired
   On floors of mirrored stone,
As when those floors with her assumed
   The shine of sun on moon –
Those courtesies on borrowed lights,
   That shone from her and were
Embroideries in marble
   And lace spun of air!

What wind has blown those lights away
   And shorn the polished stone,
Among a storm of thorn-boughs;
   Where broken years have grown
To less than her grave gentleness;
   And yet the books declare:
His dream survives and shelters
That tenant of air.

BELOVED OF NOBLES

Over the limestone mountains,
Where rain-blown roads run wild,
By limestone green in the moonlight
I've seen through a ghostly wind
Strange princes from Glen Naefin –
Like horse lords from Mayo –
On geldings, proudly riding,
With bridles of shot gold.

Yes, princes in withered brightness
Rode in a heaving crowd,
While cavalcades of ladies
Trooped swiftly with no sound,
And pale eyes in sharp faces
Glazed by, when O, I looked
On large fringed eyes of hazel
In one I deeply loved!

Her hair – a clustered helmet
Chin-strapping her calm face –
Sheltered a flame, her person
Nurtured since earthly days,
So pure in her dinted bosom –
Light-spiking the dim air –
Raising by its reflection
Love-dreams in each lean face.

Ah, who'd not follow her saddle
Among such airy forms?
Although their fiery paddocks
Are green mounds under thorn;
And so I watched them canter
Until, where roads run wild,

They plunged, through clouds that wandered
Out of a sleeping wind.

THE VISION OF BLACK GILLIBERD
(After his study of Celtic Art in early Christian Ireland)
To A.E.

While waves were glazed with silence
Beneath each shadow's weight,
The still-house in Grass Island
Kept sleep on me last night;
And there, when souls from heaven
Came softly through my sleep,
One dressed in blue mist led me
Through fields of meal and mead.

From black lands we rowed over
The sacred river Boyne,
To saints who gamely sported,
While bagpipes cried with joy
Beside four walking Beauties –
Rich cloaks over their loins,
Cloaks circled with laced serpents
Snared by their own silk coils.

Ah, there's no waste of music:
I saw the Paschal sun
Dance when a hearty psalm-tune
Was step-danced on a drum;
Even the Hazel of Knowledge
(Sworded by fiery tongues
Once moulded to anvil music)
Blossomed again in song.

Cut-stone rang with the Lord's name,
Brass eagles sang His glees,
The fingered leaves of laurel
Were folded with His peace;
Inks ran to praise His knowledge,

While His own scribe adorned
Stags sheltering in a forest
Of their own legs and horns.

And there I passed old craftsmen,
Whose knowing hands have honed –
From carven colours on parchment –
God's thought in dreaming stone,
All living in God's guildhall
(Praised be their noble souls!)
Stone artists, bardic builders,
Weavers of airy gold.

O fierce minds welded to glory
And tuned as one holy bell,
Too soon each blue hill before you
Sank from my mind, until
Each angled and arklike abbey –
White-washed as a green aired star –
Grew paler ... and there I dallied
Alone in the gathering dark;

Alone and the thin grass blowing
Soft frost by a ghostly lake;
Alone, but once a lost soul –
Naked as any snail –
Looked on me through the dark air,
And on his iceberg throne
I looked, and saw his dead face ...
And that face was my own!

THE REPENTANCE OF BLACK GILLIBERD

Now that the branch of melody breaks
In green against bare Lent
And drifts of heaven crowd Saint Patric's hill,
Without the blessings of black ash
In pure fire I repent
Of frailties in a bardic will.

For I have diced in withered towns
The true coin of the sun,
And wasted crafts when plying at my ease
The trickster's mental algebra
Of nods and winks, with one
Who brought no harvest to our knees.

Men from the road's blue mouth know well
Thoughts housed too long grow pale,
Without hostilities from wind and rain;
Yet moss and rheumy candlelight
Were mine, until fierce hail
Fell scolding on my window pane.

At one with such wild messengers,
Born of a hardy race,
I bear a spirit lit with mountain wind;
And thus unlettered, may the years
Most weather-beaten, trace
A chiselled scripture on my mind.

So here I leave to twilight pools
The forgeries of light,
While Spring is ousting Lent from bough and bone
And for pure commerce with the sun
I climb above the night,
That preys on mounds of holy stone.

Where others wear the red knee-caps
Of penitence, O may
The nettles' green teeth fall beneath my shoe,
And to this well of shining song
Bring fiery lime, I pray
O voice of mountains, lightning and dew.

THE FINDINGS: AN EPILOGUE

And should your heirs, dear readers, poach among
These holdings – when they're turbary and gorse –
If Pegasus were here they'll find his dung;
If not, the sawdust of that hobbyhorse
On which I skelpt and thought in blind delight
It scaled on wings – because my wits took flight!

THE LARK IN PURE LIGHT

Straining towards you, sky of the purest June:
Like the odd lark, freed from the weight of night
Ascending and soaring, juggling itself in a tune
Into pure air it arises and through the pure light
Raving it goes; what's heard in the song of a ghost
Even as I am heard, stained by unearthly dew
Winging, singing, ever losing myself in the most
Noble, majestic, O magnificent you.

SLEEP SONG

Lull, lullaby, all is still and the sea lakes are
Stretching the light of daytime towards the first star –
Stretching the grey light on me; and your child at rest,
Snuggling the flush of sleep on my troubled breast.

You, gentle love, I would rather have here at ease;
You, whose strong love did anoint my limbs with peace;
You, O outlawed love, not a priest, not a ghostly thief
Dare take you now from my thought that's lockjawed by grief.

What peace of mind can you have, love? Ah why not go
Wear down your spade to the butt till sweat quenches your woe,
Yes, wear down your black grief, like many a love-crazed man
Who wrenched grass out of his pain in some barren glen.

Go where you will, sacred life, you're my very own;
My breath, my breasts, they are full of you, you alone;
So, marked till death with your likeness my starved womb groans
Since you're still nailed in love onto my four bones ...

Lull, lullaby, lullaby, lulla, lullaby.

THE RING MAKER

Through you, whose hands have wrought the airy gold
Of crosses and cold elemental cups
For those whose lips kiss God, the stars this night
Draw near; O may they bless your forge, your fire,
Your flashing anvil and may they light upon
That morsel of raw metal you weld to song.

White smith, in all your living life you need
The blessing of the heavens most tonight
That limber finger, supple wrist may beat
All Ireland's graces to an inch of light
In chaste design, purer than any hymn
Inscribed by angel quills on pastured skin.

THE LITTLE FIELD OF BARLEY

Since Michaelmas I know they're saying that I'm a
changling, not a youth;
They haven't a thought of how I'm flayed to madness
like a hapless lout –
Yes, flayed by love of a thorough-bred lady for whom
grass listened when evening came;
Ah, she the clergy won't defame – her name lies sealed
within my mouth!

Of well-sprung women she's the spine that bears all
brightness, that I swear;
I've seen the skin shine through her coat when not a
comb could hold her hair;
And towards her hips her body seemed a corner of the
barley field –
But there's the crop she'll never yield – so I'll not
wield the flail elsewhere.

Look at me now! Since she has left, beside my hearth I
know I've grown
More skinned than winter till the wind can make its
bagpipes of my bones;
Here crickets talk, but that's poor song for one who
sought the bark of seals –
Here snipe with glint of light twist past—hell blast
them, my last shot is thrown.

If you draw secrets from the wind, O little birds – that
neatly leap
From twig to twig – you've heard my cries, but these
are secrets you must keep,
Until in far flights you shall find her, dreaming of me
at twilight time, –

Then sing: though broken in my mind, I'll seek her in
unquiet sleep.

Rhymes from a Limemaker

The fields, last night, were lost in brightness;
And under a fierce moonlight
The limekiln's throat wheezed with a fire
That burned the blue stones white;
And I was parched; and warping with lime
I sought, when all was still,
The Rath of the Candles that had wet apples
As I passed to the kiln.

I ran by the cross-roads of the unchristened,
Through bright fields – and nearing the rath,
Softly on soft air, words of a strange gaiety
Played to and fro on my path;
Then out of that bright air, shapes suddenly marched
Of straight men and maids, two by two;
In a glance they were gone – but a smell of munched apples
Lay over the unscattered dew.

Ah, more than the lime then thickened my tongue;
So up on the rath's still air
I sought for those apples, seen with the last sunset,
And found – not an apple there;
Just then the lake below gave a laugh
And the wood was nudged by a wind –
For the Rath of the Candles has still got its apples,
But are they for human-kind?

EXILES FROM SILENCE

Surely to-night the lost ebb of bloodties
Moves you, draws you – poor earthly shadows
From out of numb uncharted darkness –
Hearth-wards, my father and O my gay brother.

Ah, to meet you! I feel your far grey gaze leaning
Behind me; your yearnings weigh down my eyelids;
Yes, tremulously we await each other,
Hailed by our one common tongue of silence.

And so from your shy communion, on me
The pale mysteries delicately alight,
As Midnight Mass dreams towards a lone pine
Aerial, sapping the strains of *Silent Night*.

ACKNOWLEDGEMENTS

Sincere thanks to both the board of Poetry Ireland and all the staff of Poetry Ireland for their support in publishing this book, along with the Gray family, Higginsbrook, and Aidan Gray for his work with Dardis Clarke in compiling this selection. Thanks to the estate of Sean O'Sullivan, the estate of Harry Kernoff, the National Gallery of Ireland and the Abbey Theatre for their assistance and support, and to Alan Hayes, Arlen House, for responding so enthusiastically and practically to remembering and recalling Dardis Clarke and F.R. Higgins respectively.

The publisher would like to acknowledge the dedication of Joe Woods in seeing this book completed, and in editing the text and writing the introduction, in challenging conditions in an almost internet-free area.